WHEN THE ALARM SOUNDS

The Life and Daily Struggles of an EMT, Fireman, and Mother

by

Joseph E. Fowler Jr. (MSCJA)

DORRANCE
PUBLISHING CO
EST 1920
PITTSBURGH, PENNSYLVANIA 15238

Dorrance Publishing Co
585 Alpha Drive
Suite 103
Pittsburgh, PA 15238
Visit our website at www.dorrancebookstore.com

ISBN: 979-8-89341-382-3
eISBN: 979-8-89341-881-1

Dedication

This book was written with the mind, body, and soul of a true hero. She never thinks of herself in the time of someone else's needs. A veteran, a wife and mother, an inspiration, an EMT.

INTRODUCTION

When the Alarm Sounds

A look at the people who will face a challenge every day and win

They go through their normal days as moms, bank tellers, volunteer workers and other members of society hoping it doesn't happen during dinner or a school play or even sex with their spouse, but in the back of their heads they know it can and will happen whether they are ready or not.

The men and women who choose this profession must be a strange group from the start to delve into another profession to which one sees the circle of life almost every day they hit the streets and highways to save the people they don't know and maybe a few they do.

From the back seat as it were, I had the opportunity to such work a few years ago as a member of the local fire department but my other job, the U.S. Army, put a halt to that for me but my other half jumped in with both feet; she loves everything about the life as an EMT or Emergency Medical Technician. The training is constant and like any other job politics still runs deep in a world to which those that hit the streets need to be ready 24/7 when the alarm sounds and when they gather at the station to prep for a trip into the unknown.

On the average day "on the rig," as they call it, it's prep work on the rig, making sure they have everything a crew will need to save a life or two, but when it doesn't happen it's cool because it's just a dry run, as they call it. As a volunteer for a job as dangerous as this is a paycheck seems too little, but with calls times pay per trip it can be a nice check for primarily volunteer work, and yes, a few volunteers who seem to be money hungry and that's all they are in it for, which is not what this type of work is all about. They do get something for all the time, effort, education and training they must go through along with recertify every few years or so, to continue saving the lives of others.

We will put on the gear and hit the streets of a small town where the EMTs are most needed and try to understand their silly season or AKA the wintertime, when people from other nearby states pass through without thinking that driving in California is vastly different from driving in Wyoming and on a major highway to which the winds can measure 100 mph, ground blizzards, black ice, vehicle and truck crashes on a regular basis. We will explore the constant calls on the radio, personal cell phones, and constant chatter about a call whether good or bad.

They face the challenges of getting to a scene within minutes and having an open mind about what they are about to see or put their hands in or on, all members are to be able to be flexible to work all parts of the rig while staying cool under pressure.

When the Alarm Sounds

As it happens, I know a few of them personally because they are my neighbors, people you wouldn't look at twice, if you were to think of an emergency crew doing one of the most dangerous jobs in the world. In an average rig, there are five people ready to hit the road when duty calls: the lead EMT, a driver, and two paramedics. Each job is very important in itself and to the other members of the rig, the lead EMT must have his/her crew ready to handle anything at the scene and sometimes not, and properly access what is in front of them and offer the right medical short-term attention and transport the victim to the hospital, the driver must be able to driver in any weather with lights and sirens wailing in every direction for all to hear and make sure the rig is up to date on all maintenance needs and is ready at all times.

The two paramedics in the back of the rig are there to comfort the victim and to offer him/her medical attention while getting them to the nearest hospital if they need it. Sometimes a victim will refuse to go to the hospital and a crew member must get them to sign a waiver stating that they refused medical attention on their own accord, and that if medical attention is needed later the crew of that rig is not liable for his/her future medical needs. The lead EMT is in contact with the local police department dispatcher to get the information of an accident, and if the rig crew is close enough to the scene they are call out by their rig number and they hit the road.

The lead EMT, her name is Anna, she is married with two children, she met her husband at a chance football game years ago. After he left the military, they moved away from the big city life for cleaner air and more animals than a zoo running wild outside their modest Wyoming home.

Grace, Anna's number two, is a very eager housewife with kids of her own and looking for a challenge in her own life after a few lifeless jobs in other markets and has been living in our small town longer than Anna, but bested Anna the minute they first spoke. Around the same age, they both found something they can do as friends and neighbors. One of the paramedics, named Trudy, is willing to do what it takes to become an EMT, but her personal life is a mess and she is looking for answers in all the wrong places. Asking for help and not using it hurts all those around her. And the last member of Anna's crew is May, an older lady divorced twice and retired but must live and act young to feel useful to those around her. She is not quite the paramedic she needs to be but simply refuses to ask for help or step away from the rig so others younger can take her place.

On a typical day things are slow at the station, with normal prep work or trying to set up training for this rig crew, Anna is the one really doing that part. She has mastered all the paperwork to memory and can tell someone how to use the computer from over the phone. Anna is tall for the lead EMT; most people think she was a basketball player in her younger days. She was but she hated it; looking like a jock doesn't mean you are one. Grace has never left the state of Wyoming in her life and loves to hunt with her husband and kids; it's the one thing they all can agree on doing when it gets cold. Trudy also has two kids and is not sure if she wants to live on her own or to be a wife to a man who's not quite sure he wants a wife and kids to take care of himself. Trudy joined the rig crew to clear her mind while helping others to which she is very good at and other people tell her so, she is good at giving meds to those who are afraid of needles and has a calming effect in a stressful situation. Anna tells her all the time, "I need you by my side out there, so stay focused for me and you'll go places." May thinks she's ready to oversee the rig and its crew and she could except for one thing, stage fright. Classroom work or a training session is not the real thing but in May's mind it is. A practice dummy can't bleed out, scream in pain, beg for meds because they need a fix, or help an officer remove a victim stuck in a smashed vehicle in the wind and cold of another harsh Wyoming winter.

And lastly there is Lisa B, an ex-schoolteacher with supermodel looks. She too has a family and is looking for something better out of life than where she is right now, her kids are growing up and the house will be empty soon, so she decided to join the EMTs and put her energy to use for something good. With Lisa B's good looks, one would never think that she has a mean streak the size of Kansas, so it's best to stay on her good side, and that includes victims she comes across at an accident.

With a full staff of ten people, five for a rig and the other five for intermediate, extra drivers and trainees the area to which they work is called "Frontier Medicine." That's what it's called from the powers that be who run this state, which is small in population, so some people think that we live in an area that doesn't need an ambulance service and a crew of five ready when the alarm sounds to do their jobs. These people are nameless until they are needed and that comes every winter on the highways of Wyoming.

FRONTIER MEDICINE

Frontier Medicine never stops. On the day in question last year it was Christmas Day, just about to open presents and it happened, the alarm sounds and they are off and running on a holiday when the conditions are so bad it's almost unbearable, winds at 30-40 mph, 6-8 inches of soft snow in a rig with max speed of 100 mph, and the patient is an 84-year-old woman with an unknown hip injury. Anna curses out loud to me as she in a panic looks for clothes that are appropriate for the task at hand.

Minutes later she's out the door with no plan in mind if the patient goes from bad to worse within minutes of driving the 45-plus minutes to the hospital. The roads are winding, icy, snow-covered layers of unsafe asphalt 44 miles of white-knuckle driving for the driver and crew with a patient in tow. Anna is back to active duty after two months laid up from a partially torn left shoulder muscle, to which she hated hearing calls on the radio and not being able to respond, not having the mental rush of saving a life.

Anna is working with a skeleton crew because of the holiday, people she may or may not know much about but still working as a unit to save a life in harsh conditions almost no one should be out in. Wyoming is one of those states to where people either leave because of the cold harsh winters or pass through on their way to somewhere warm, so the people that stay behind are more than tough enough to handle what comes their way, a state with more animals than people, the open frontier makes you (us) tougher than most. I still hope of leaving just because I was born in the big city so that's what I know, but since being out here for close to ten years I'm coming around, while Anna loves every minute of living out here and the kids seem to be okay with living amongst the wild.

The work is as harsh as the winters but there is a time when the snow melts, the animals come out from hiding, schools are closer to closing for the summer, it's called the summertime but the drivers on the highways are just as bad because the road speed is 80 mph, so in most states it's 65-75 mph. With that extra speed comes more dangerous drivers who are not used to driving that fast and with the winds that can average close to 100 mph in some areas of the state, truckers get turned over very easily, even with warnings over the radio and TV people still don't listen till it's too late and they end up in a ditch on the side of the road or worse, the hospital, because they do not listen and they think they know more than a Wyoming winter.

Anna is in contact with another crew if they can't get to a scene because they may be too far away, the crew's cover areas ranging from 10 miles to 100 miles away, so sometimes crews must or should work together to get a patient to the hospital in a timely manner. Some of the other crews aren't as efficient as Anna's full-time crew, some say even better, they are more knowledgeable about new and advanced medicines and procedures that the average victim may not know. When the weather breaks most EMTs and drivers have such classes to stay abreast of what's new in the world of new medicine and procedures EMTs must now know and use. These such classes come out of each crew member's pocket, ranging from $25-$150, and in places not close to home in any way, so travel and finances play a part in who is to get to use this newfound knowledge and apply it in the time of need.

The team, of a lead EMT, an Intermediate, a Driver, and a 1ST Responder, and if available 1 trainee, make up the crew on a rig, and if you're on duty that day you go out when the alarm sounds, but if you're not up to it for almost any reason you can get bumped from that call, which is up to the lead EMT and/or the Intermediate. "Jumping Calls" is an act that is frowned upon but happens when someone off duty gets into the rig, which someone on duty must go back home and not be able to assist as part of his/her original duty.

There is no real recourse for "Jumping Calls" when asked not to do this, a few people on Anna's crew have done this to her in the most recent of days. She, the Lead EMT, was very hot under the collar about this because her crew left her on the side of the road on that wintery day. She left a universal note for all to see about this, and if it happens again to her or anyone on her crew someone would get fired for committing an offensive act while under her charge.

When "Jumping Calls" happens on a frequent manner losing call time can happen, this means being taken off your shift. People must remember that Anna is a paid volunteer who works fulltime and considers this her full-time job. Unlike other members of her crew who have another job to rely on, Anna is not working for the money, outcome not income toward helping others is what Anna lives by and she hopes others would do the same. Some people want the money but don't have the mental capacity to be a hands-on EMT, and thus making it hard on those who are out there to make a difference in other people's lives.

This job while seemingly easy is not, getting up at all hours of the night, getting dressed in pounds of gear, no coffee, and hitting the road with your crew may be exciting until you arrive at the scene and it's a mother and her baby pinned under a tractor-trailer because they were driving too fast in the Wyoming winter without being prepared to stop if an accident happened in front of them, and now it is them. How does one react at a scene when it's someone you know, or even a neighbor from down the street, to which Anna has had the mis-pleasure of doing just that…. The walk in the door says it all to me and not bother her for an hour or so until she comes to me and lets me know what happened and who it was and then we let it go. Enough said.

A Wyoming Education

A Wyoming education is vastly different from all other EMT crews throughout the United States, one would think that the ultimate career path for an EMT would be to become a Paramedic, flight or otherwise, but that is the mindset of the few, not the many. Anna is one of those people who sets a goal and does her best to get there, from her bosses Anna's crew should only work a minimum of 24 hours per month in any fashion they want: 24 hrs. per month, 1 call, or 1 meeting or any combination. Yes, you can work more but the minimum is not a lot to ask for in relation to other crews in other parts of the country.

In Wyoming, an EMT's card lasts two years and is very easy to recertify and keep your card active so one can continue to work. There is no retesting of any kind, continuing education credits are up to the individual person currently on a rig, the pay is minimal at best $1 per hour and/or $50 per call, so many calls can equal a nice paycheck but not very often (it's not enough to live on, if you were thinking of it). Some crew members who don't want any money because they really want the volunteer aspect to be true for them will give back any money they have earned while helping others.

One can even donate his/her pay for the same reasons as stated above as a show of respect to those who take EMT, Paramedic life serious and not a part-time hobby. Wyoming has many fewer things to offer by way of hospitals, more efficient hospitals with surgeons on hand, level-one trauma centers to handle drastic events quickly, or doctors on hand and access a victim to see if he/she needs to be air lifted to Denver at 55k per hour for the pilot. Other states have more and do more to help the EMT and Paramedic to do their jobs better by offering hands-on training, film sessions, cross-training, and better pay to keep them around for more than a year or two.

States have Trauma Conferences every year in various locations like Salt Lake City, Gillette, Cheyenne, and this year Las Vegas. These conferences aren't free so one has to qualify for a grant if possible or start to gather those funds long before the conference is to take place and the price can range from $500 or more, not to include room and travel plans (weather pending). At these conferences EMTs and Paramedics share new and/or updated information one part of the country may not know about or have seen in action, there is some side recruiting going on if one area of the country has heard of an EMT or driver doing exceptional work and tries to get him/her to move and work for them with the promise of better everything. People can even do ride-alongs to see what it's like in another rig and the set-up of meds compared to your own, and after all the meet-and-greets have ended they unwind with a few cocktails and share ideas with other staffers. One must believe that all these things will help an EMT become the best person they can, but we already know we all have different agendas for doing something whether positive or negative, and to me I see all this up close and private when things go wrong or bad or both for that matter and not having a say truly is humbling.

The crews may be small but their intentions are good, they for the most part are dedicated to the job and their craft, helping others when they can, or putting someone in their place if they need to, and sometimes it should. As of late Trudy has had a change of heart when it comes to working on a rig and becoming a full-time EMT or driver, her personal life is in turmoil, and she thought that time with Anna, Grace, and the others would send her in the right direction, but she seems determined to do her own thing and leave her friends standing by while she makes up her mind as to what she wants to do in life.

Trudy is one of those kinds of women who seems to enjoy drama or needs to be the center of attention for all the wrong reasons, in her mind of course, but she needs to prioritize because of her two kids, a five-year-old and a teenager with a teenager's mindset (me vs. the world or I know everything, I'm 18). Anna and Trudy were once joined at the hip when we first moved here because back then Trudy needed advice from a stable marriage and positive influence from people, older and wiser than she. Anna thought work of this magnitude would turn Trudy around, things started out great, extra hours learning procedures, how to handle needles, up-set patience, and everything else that comes with working as a fulltime EMT.

But things turned for Trudy a few months ago when her soon-to-be ex-husband used the children as leverage against her and through the court system made the divorce so harsh for her she must stay with him, and thus he used that to verbally abuse her and the teenager to no end, so with this in hand work seemed far in the past because her mind and heart were not in it and that's not how a crew member should act when others come first.

At this point we don't know where Trudy's mind is on work or trying to decide if she wants to be married or divorced or not, so until she sorts out her private life her work life is on hold per Anna, the lead EMT.

May is altogether another type of woman and from afar seems like the type of person that must know what's going on always, passed her prime a few years ago, her reasons for wanting to be an EMT or driver is just for the knowledge of knowing "what happened today" and she may or may not have had something to do with the outcome. Retired for a few years now, she looks to stay young at heart by trying to do a volunteer job with money on her mind.

She somehow got a card as an EMT but doesn't work alone ever! She always wants to know what Anna is doing and whether if she is working today, but if left in charge of a rig or crew at an accident she is lost, but will never admit it to herself or others, at one point she told Anna that she's only doing this because she may miss out on today's happenings, which makes her feel young at heart. There is no way to just ask may to step down without a fight, so the others will have to just wait her out. Less is more sometimes, if the person(s) is better than what she should work with now and possible in the future. Too many excuses can/should get you kicked off the rig or service for not doing the simplest of tasks when on call for a month at a time, losing call time or being taken off shift is the only control a Lead EMT or station manager has.

This Is Too Much

Just like any other job, people can burn out from what they see and do on a regular basis, this can be too much for some so they find a way to cope, they mentally say I can't do this anymore, the stresses of going to scene after scene of death, PTSD, depression, reclusiveness, frustrating, criticize yourself and your abilities, while shutting yourself off from others and possible suicidal thoughts. Some people say the worst patients are doctors, nurses, EMTs, paramedics and others that work in the medical field because they know all the technical terms, medicines, and possible outcomes from which the regular person would not.

Some people would rather step away from working as an EMT or driver for the greater good, because of their abilities and to fight amongst other EMTs or drivers, or one's ability to do his/her job when requested to do so in a timely manner. There are some patients called "Frequent Flyers" because of their ability to get high through the abilities of EMTs and hospital staff once they arrive. This becomes old hat after a few trips of picking up the same people or person only looking to get high.

"Don't let her touch me" is sometimes told to the EMTs by older people who are stuck in the old ways and traditions, and they seem to like Anna and most of her crew except for May, she's as old as some of the patients she's trying to save. May wants things she can't have, like the power to be in charge, the knowledge others have, and having the knowledge to say, "I can't do this, can you help?" May is at the bottom of the food chain, and very eager not to lead in any way but her own, she relies on Anna way too much and it is now becoming a pain in Anna's ass. This sentiment goes throughout the town, people hear of her bad reputation and want nothing.

Anna and Grace once told me that one accident scene was as harsh as could be because when they got to the scene, "they were all gone, the whole family," meaning the entire family from Utah was killed because they weren't wearing seatbelts and an average speed of the car they were in was nearly 85 mph. The mother went through the windshield, her son was stuck in the vehicle by the oncoming truck almost cut in half, the other two in the back seat were killed on impact of both vehicles hitting each other with such force. This took a toll on Anna and Grace, who were both on the scene as it came across the radio, for assistance.

Anna told all the higher-ups that she needed some time to herself over what she had to deal with at that scene, Grace too needed time to decompress, seeing life-and-death acts on the side of the road is something not for the fainthearted. Her chain of command gave Anna and Grace beef over what they saw and how not to bring death home to their personal lives. When something like this happens and you're first on the scene, someone should call the coroner and inform him/her to come prepared to find a body, or someone in parts because the scene was so bad, to officially call the time of death to the victim or victims. One hopes this doesn't happen but when it does they all defuse in their own way, to which we spoke about already, but when it passes most EMTs are ready to get back into it.

"I'm back" is their cry as they look to get back into the action of saving lives, working as a unit, learning new things from other areas of the country. And if they are too depressed and want to leave that life they can with no regrets. They will be nervous and excitement and looking for a good outcome the 1st time around back on the streets. Maybe things will be different when they return, maybe the chain of command will have formed to let others know about the changes that have/will be taken place for the good of the unit, crews on the rig and the future for that matter, but that's just wishful thinking on my part, for I'm just an outsider looking at this job of mostly women being braver than anyone can expect.

When the alarm sounds, they must stop their private lives to save someone they may or may not know, clear weather or bad, near home or far (the county lines) in every direction, whether they feel up to it at the time or not, knowing that they are coming to save a life is all a victim is looking forward to pending on the type of accident in the first place, or if it is too minor to go to the hospital or sign a refusal form. There have been days when a crew arrives to a scene and the only thing they can do is call the coroner and take the body or bodies away either before or after they call "time of death" to make it official for the records and the family of the victim(s).

One would think that even the coroner would feel bad for the victims every time they get called to a scene and it's never the same, never a positive outcome along with all the things that go on after the body is in the morgue. Not sure if the EMTs or drivers want to end up in the medical field working with dead bodies all the time, this would make very bad bedtime stories or conversations over dinner.

Helping the cops and vice versa leads to a good reputation while out on the streets because they almost interact with each other and are looking for the same thing, someone to help or someone to lock up and/or send to the hospital. Police arrive on some scenes to enter a home to clear it of drugs, weapons, dead bodies, etc. It would be very hard for EMTs to work if they have to pick up a victim to later find out that he/she was wanted by the police on varies charges and while in their care something out of the norm happens. An average day for an EMT or driver may send them out on the road more than three times in a day, so pretty much they have time to restock the rig and get back out there, refocused and ready to go.

The rig is a portable hospital of sorts, it has a bed for patients, loads of medicines, gauze pads of all sizes and lots of other things I can't remember or pronounce but very much needed in time of an emergency. The rig should be properly maintained for all seasons and be ready to go at a moment's notice, the driver should be able to concentrate on where the accident is and not if the rig has a mechanical problem or needs something done to stay ready. They only have two rigs but four firetrucks in case of a fire and two transport vehicles to assist other rigs having to take patients to some place other than a local hospital.

From the families' view they see daring parents doing a job that they love to do, the kids hear the calls on the radio, ask questions an EMT would ask and be concerned about the timeframe to which they will return, not knowing all the details of a call but sounding concerned when they come home. The daughter Daisy, a very active 13-year-old who wants to follow in Anna's footsteps when she is old enough, scared and excited over the fact that Anna can/has the ability to save a life, not knowing one single thing about the victim because the hospital is so far away and the victim needs help right now…so it's Anna to the rescue!

Her son Michael is very inquisitive about her job and wants her to call home at every off chance she must stay longer than two, that's his version of worrying, he's not too expressive in the form of words directly to Anna but calling her while at work can sometimes be a pain. Even the dogs react to the alarm when it goes off because they too know Anna will be leaving and not knowing when she will be coming back and thus the reaction every time she does walk back through the door.

I try to stay awake listening to the radio when she's out there, knowing some of the details of her job, I find it interesting too, the stories she tells me after it is all over for the day and we are unwinding over a few drinks or that eerie silence of something too emotional, scary, or deadly to talk about, but I wait until she's in a better mood to talk about the situation that made her and her crew very nervous and/or upset over the fact that they may have had to save someone they knew or the victim died and again the crew knew of them.

From the second seat in all this is Grace, what if Anna was gone and Grace would have to take her place, would things be the same, rig wise? Is Grace ready? Is she learning anything or more than Anna or just the basic stuff, with a few training sessions added in? Personal life aside, Grace says yes to being able to handle being in charge. The chain of command is something that falls on deaf ears on some rigs due to a few problems that they fail to tackle head on versus letting it stew and becoming worse in the long run. Favoritism seems to run wild and free, even with a Lead EMT running the rigs, certain people seem to think they either work when they want to, or don't have to listen to others. Board members offer no discipline either because they all live somewhere other than the small town we call home. In some professions like doctors and lawyers there are such laws like HIPPA that allow certain things to remain private between two parties, EMTs and drivers must follow such laws, they know these laws going to work every day and that the things they see and do must stay within the rig personal. Anna has had members of her crew break these laws and yet no penalty ensues, along with call jumping and no floating schedules for working on holidays, these are some of the real problems Anna has to deal with along with never getting a minute to herself when she needs it, because certain members of her crew fear working alone or being the lead EMT without Anna present. This is not most people's dream job, but a stepping stone to something else in another town, those young enough to do so, not those who are about to become senior citizens or retire from the workforce altogether.

Traveling Out West

We were in the U.S. Navy together for a few years without really knowing one another, her department and mine did work in close quarters for most of the time, the information her department obtained helped my department keep us afloat, meaning a ship's driver or helmsman in Navy terms. She was dating someone else and so was I but we were put together by our friends who thought that we'd make a great couple. She had gotten out of the service first, then me a few years later, and with a baby and a toddler in tow we headed out west to Wyoming from Michigan, the Big Three was closing along with all its major suppliers, which funneled down to me, even though I had get finished college, looking for a job was harder than one can expect from a job market that was leaving the U.S. faster than one could count.

Things were looking bleak for a time or two but just when we had run out of applications to fill out the Wyoming Department of Corrections came to our rescue, they were recruiting in Michigan to where they knew the people were looking for work but under some rules, like relocation on your own dime, but we had two things needed for relocation: time and the ability to move, so on to the Greyhound Bus station for me, while the family came a few weeks after me by car. Landing in Wyoming was culture shock to us, but for me it was especially hard to adjust to a place where there are more animals than people, the small town we call home has 840 people and those numbers are getting smaller by the year as high schoolers look beyond the divided highway for scenes of life.

While we have a high schooler looking to end his high school career soon, he has no plans on leaving this small town due to his mental handicap but others look to go far and as fast as possible. This is where small-town living can be a plus because we have outside education, have traveled the world as sailors, and served our country, and are still young enough to raise a family, and watch them grow up all around us. There isn't much to do as a young person in this town, those of us stuck in the middle made due with the things around us like, the fire department or EMT/driver or something else out of town, we got lucky enough to try out the fire department 1st as we were new to town, I couldn't stay on long because I was still serving in the Army and it kept me busy but Anna liked it right away but the chain of command was changing so she decided to move on before it got shut done for good.

As it would have it, Anna fit the EMT profile like a glove (unlike O.J.), she was eager to get started with a new career and starting from the bottom she took to it quickly and within a few years, many classes, on-the-job training, original accident scenes, and asking many questions about people and medicine, Anna is now the lead EMT in town, and her crew still can't operate without her around. Anna's mom is a retired nurse so they both know the ins and outs of medicine to a degree, Anna could be a nurse if she really applied herself, but the cost of being a full-time doctor is something she would have to consider strongly before the age of 50, she's 46.

Anna and I spent a total of 17 years in the U.S. Navy, that's where we met, on the same ship but in different departments, but they did coincide with each other: Operations and Deck seamanship, the information we get from Ops helps us from crashing into another ship or running aground due to bad/inclement weather. Since we were in such close quarters while working it wasn't that hard to find something in common with a coworker, but we were both seeing other people at the time and had no interest in one another at that time, but things would change over the next few weeks.

Since we were working together (sort of) our friends thought it would be an excellent idea to put us together, so one long day for both of us, to which we were dating other people, she was dating a bully with a temper, and the reason I know this firsthand is because she was attacked in the NCO club for enlisted sailors, and just before the police arrived, he had run off to not get caught but she waited to tell them her side of the story and at the same time I was arriving to get away from my long-distance relationship from my girlfriend in Scranton-Wilkes Barre, the western part of Pennsylvania, through as many drinks as possible.

Our chance meeting turned out to be good for both of us in the long run, since we were both having a day with our current relationships and they were certainly over at this point, we both had not thought of each other for guidance but our friends did, they thought a change was indeed better, and as luck would have it, they were right. First finding out that we were on the same ship and working close to one another was a plus, we could see each other almost every day while out to sea, and that did help pending on whether we had wives or husbands back home. We had each other for six months and it was great not being alone in times of need but liberty call was even more great because we coupled up by departments and it was an unwritten rule as to whom you could date, Ops and Deck department had paired up and the couples seemed to fit, Anna and I along with several others, it was nice.

This was the first time we had been on a Med-Cruise together without really knowing each other, some called what we were doing a "Med-Cruise Marriage," to which couples (really married or not) would dating while on the Med-Cruise but break up a few weeks before heading home to Virginia Beach, Virginia. Things were not great for other couples that had to split up due to real feelings coming out, I gave Anna the option of leaving me beforehand, but she stayed by my side as if we had been together for years on end, this is how you know "she's the one for me" and I her, for that matter we stayed together without really asking the other, "What are we doing as a couple?" Things were great with us but the big news was 10 lbs. and 28 ins. away.

I was about to leave the ship soon; married couples weren't allowed to stay on the same ship since a spouse would worry about his/her spouse over his/her job and thus things become complicated. We are a mixed couple and not sure how her parents were going to take it knowing that they were about to become grandparents, and another thing…we had nothing in common, until we were all in the same room, Anna's parents are Air Force veterans, her mom loves to cook, is a nurse, her dad was an electrician and a grocery store owner heading toward retirement. Anna made the surprise visit and announcements over dinner with all of us pausing in that awkward silence until Mom-in-law asked a simple question: boy or girl? And when will we return from our visit with their grandson in tow? After that, things were fine with both her parents, at my house things were cool but coming from a different direction, they were a lot more relaxed and open meaning a six-foot white girl did fit right in with a house full of kids and strippers that my mom managed for more than ten years, and back in the 1980s things were much more fun at least in our household.

We met in a chance encounter though others but we stayed together for the love we have for each other that has lasted for close to 25 years so far, we had different ideas for our own futures, I wanted a career in Law Enforcement since having two degrees in that field it seemed to be a good fit. Anna's plans, to the best of my knowledge, were/are to be an EMT full time and she is making strides to do just that, lots of schooling is required and seminars from across the country and most of them aren't free and that's where I come in, giving her the money to travel and making sure she's safe at the same time. If you ask ten kids today what they want to be when they grow up few if any will say EMT, you never hear about them doing something heroic but it does happen almost every day in their world, I get to see things others cannot or will not ever see when they come home from a scene, EMTs are in the medical field for just the right reasons, not for the money and/or the lack thereof....

Other professions see the money first as a lead to what could be.... EMTs see the work as a stepping stone to other medical professions like a trauma nurse, surgical nurse, flight nurse or even a doctor if they want to endure all the schooling. The hours are long, there is never a real thank-you from the people they save, or the chain of command in which they work for, I don't see how they picked a thankless job and are great at it, get up every day and commit to saving others. Anna herself had to deal with being alone when I was headed overseas back in 2009, we being the Army was stationed down in Texas, getting ready to go over when I tore my ACL training, I knew things for me were over when they took my weapon away and sent me to the south side of the base to where people waited for medical discharges, a ride to another base for more training, weapons detail and/or training and even night vision training or more over all the above. I had to break the news to her over the phone to which was good and bad at the same time, I was not going overseas but I'm not coming home just yet either, my injury left me on the base for surgery and recovery time of a year or more with rehab included.

I had to do the leg work myself in the form of finding my own doctor to do the surgery I needed, the doctor I had spoken with was green in that area and told me to my face he had not done more than three ACL surgeries and wasn't sure if he was the right person for me, with that I was sent on my way back to Wyoming to do all the things the doctors in Texas didn't do.

This was a surprise to Anna, who thought I'd be home for good with no apparent injuries to be taken care of, this was not true. My surgical journey started a few weeks from returning from Texas, my first was for a torn ACL, which took a year to recover from even if I wasn't a soldier.

While recovering from one surgery, things got worse by the way of an infection in my knee to which the doctors took two-plus years to confirm to the point where a pick-line had to be inserted into my arm with a lead over my heart to force the infection out and the medicine in, I was glad Anna is an EMT or I would have had to drive the four hundred miles every week round trip just to change the pick-line out and to clean the area of infection as well, on top of injections of Lovenox one per day for eight weeks too. This caused me to put on weight, and more than what I was used to when it came to winter weight, over 200 lbs., and I felt like it was 200 more, I'm not the fittest person in the world, but I do consider myself fit enough not to be a fat-ass.

While I was recovering a few days ahead of me Anna was doing her own of sorts, I heard that she had a heart attack due to stresses of me heading overseas to fight or so she thought, one event outweighed the other, in my mind and of course I had no idea, these are the things that were not shared with a spouse already in a stressful situation. It was mild but deeply related to my situation and knowing that I had years of surgeries ahead of my Anna could do nothing to help me but worry about the outcome of one surgery and hoping that "this will be the last one" to which it wasn't. They all worried about me but as a soldier we must only for a moment think of the unthinkable and what we are leaving behind if it happens either on the battlefield or on a surgical table with others holding your life in their hands.

Every time I went into an operating room this was on my mind and asking God to help the people helping me at the time for things to go well, but if they didn't know that I did all I could to be a good husband, father, and son that my small part of the world would be allowed to continue, and thus I would enjoy life even more than I already do and try not to let things beyond my control affect my life and family. Anna was not the real expressive type when it came to things like that, I one the other hand learned through the Army to find an outlet to stress, so, I write, in journals, scraps of paper, or even just doodling to get my thought out of my head and on to something else other than acting on it in a negative way, to which the social workers that visit every month or so will not be surprised if I did, it's not if but when a soldier does something to himself and/or his family. Anna is a big girl and the stress of both our situations had caused her to lose some weight to almost an alarming rate and this too wasn't good for us as a family.

This would leave our children with no parents or one parent having the burden of losing the other and with years of coping in the years after, gladly we aren't at this street yet and if ever it had to happen it would kill one or both of us mentally more than physically and that would be hard for anyone to handle alone.

Dealing with Being Alone

One would think that things would be very hard for Anna and the children if I had passed on one of those operating tables over the past few years, before one such operation my youngest took a heartfelt picture of us before I was to go under the knife, we all were hoping that, that I can see and hear her crying over my lifeless body and not being able to stop for hours and having to tell the kids the same, our so-called friends would show up sadder than Anna and offering her words of condolence and hoping things would get better for her newly broken family, for Anna death was something she had to deal with in her job but when it comes to her face to face, she would be like any other person who's lost someone of 25-plus years on this earth together, we would say to each other in a joking manner, "I'd send you back, but I can't find the receipt."

We were both allowed to look but not touch when it came to others, and we both knew that we would dance with the one you love, but that's for another book some other time. I would never purposely leave Anna and the kids alone like some other dads or men pretending to be dads, someone once said, "Anyone can be a dad but it's work to be a father." I like being a husband and a father, especially to the kids I helped bring into this world. A man should keep his word to his kids because at some point you will need them when we get old and gray and need help getting to the bathroom on time or can't remember which meds to take on which days. If I happen to leave this world and Anna and the kids would really know what it's like to be alone or the road one takes to bounce back, what is the timeframe to feeling whole again?

People write their opinion about life all the time, but when is it true for you to personally feel better about the loss of a spouse, we all recover at our own pace, there's not enough time for some when it comes to things like this, while others just jump into the next best thing that comes along or the best thing right now. I think Anna would have trouble in this area after me and my youngest would be very defensive about meeting another man to take my place, she is of course a daddy's girl and I love that about her, while my son would be more isolated than he already is and would be even harder to talk to than he already is, since his mental disability would force him to think of me even more after I'm gone and would only express himself to Anna with a face full of tears when he thinks of me from time to time.

I would wonder how the kids would grow up without me around, offering advice about their lives making fun of my daughter's dates as we have expressed in the months passed in hoping to embarrass her to the point of her dates not come around at all. My kids would sorely miss the fun we had together, like duct taping her to the wall of our house, chasing her with meat while the dogs run after us too to get the meat from us, or teaching her to drive at the tender age of thirteen. I'm not sure if Anna would even date anyone at all after me because when we met it was an unpleasant day for her at the time and I approached her under a stressful situation, while dating means looking for someone to be a part of her life and she may not know how to ask or be asked to let someone into her life. I hope to never put her in that position, I'm 52 years old right now and hope to live till I hit 100, to me that's the number I'd like to hit by way of living a full life and having Anna by my side will help me achieve my goal, not sure if Anna thinks like I do when it comes to things like that but I do and it helps by living the way we want. I tried to surprise Anna with an anniversary with a unique background of sorts, she fought me tooth and nail for me to not give her anything for her birthday…but we all know the truth about that, if I don't get her something I'll hear about it till her next birthday and if I go get her something she may not like I'll hear it till her next birthday so what is a husband to do? The gift I am buying is a triple-exposed picture of her thumbprint under glass, something to which no one I know has, this is a gift others would jump for joy over, and yet she hates every aspect of it and thus a verbal fight ensued, how can a husband do both? This is a very frustrating time, so after 30 min. of silence in the car on our way back home we dropped the subject but I didn't concede the idea and a few days later she agreed to the entire process and the print is in the works.

Her friends will hear of this and blame me for not being as romantic as the next guy, and yet still want me to be romantic all the time if not more, to which this will not happen, we all know that Valentine's Day is predominantly a girl, wife, girlfriends holiday and the men concede that so we can have our holiday, aka the Super Bowl. Anna is very hard to shop for so the print I had made would last for a few years for her to enjoy and maybe a print for myself sometime down the line or if the money was right to have it done. She has told me more than once, "Don't get me anything I don't ask for," which means "I hate surprises" and I should never try to surprise her.

Anna just recently came back from another conference in Utah with some of her EMT friends to which they all used different modes of transportation instead of going together and saving some money, anyway her chain of command is planning an EMT of the year ceremony and if Anna doesn't win it, this would be a conspiracy in the form of whoever gets that award really doesn't know what the hell they are doing when it comes to being professional like Anna, all her friends and neighbors will tell you that something's wrong if she doesn't win that award.

From what I hear they are usually just a swag swop from venders across the country but this time things were different and the swag was light but the opportunities were plenty and to me that's the best part of her trips around the country to see how other EMT units are run, word of mouth is a good thing for those looking for better work in a better part of this country, many of Anna's friends don't get the pub she gets even if she doesn't want it, but secretly does. Other EMTs have heard of Anna and her abilities to do a better-than-average job as an EMT. They offer a job if she were to relocate to New Orleans or another southern state where more EMTs are needed in rural areas or big sporting events like the Super Bowl or a NASCAR event. Here in Wyoming there are no such things that big unless one counts the Cheyenne Frontier Days Rodeo in July, to which things do get out of hand after a few too many drinks and getting rejected by all the hotties in booty shorts and plaid shirts. Local hospitals in the area expect a few calls when this event takes place in late July so they are staffed with extra doctors and nurses but the EMTs will be at the event to help the injured make it to the hospital in one piece. They cover all kinds of injuries including drunks, accident victims from the rodeo, possible drunk drivers getting evaluated and released and many others. It was a super-windy day but not like no other, it was up over 50 mph and not letting up anytime soon over the next week to ten days.

The call came out over the radio around 7 A.M., a sleepy-eyed EMT looked for her version of a uniform, keys, a hat, and her big blue jacket with ten pockets, once dressed she kissed me and the kids and was out the door before I could tell her to be careful out there. The day before while out on the road going to a scene with a rookie driver, he hit the side of an 18-wheeler truck while saying he couldn't see how much room he had to get around it on the way to the scene from the start, not being one to complain to the chain of command, Anna may have re-injured her neck and/or back when they hit that truck, but not enough to cost more than $600 and a few days in the shop for the trucker.

All were back to work the very next call; Grace's real job has put her on second shift while Ann is in recovery for something taking more than two weeks to recover from. Grace and her family moved closer to Anna and her family due to her husband's job relocation, and thus Grace would be able to work more side by side with Anna to learn as much as possible because at some point Anna will have to take a step back due to various reasons like all her medical issues and stresses of work so many hours with little time off.

While on location the weather went from bad to worse, with high winds to a snowstorm only hours apart, making highway rescue help all most impossible to do, but those that are dedicated to helping others harder than ever to do. One must understand that they never stop, take a holiday, calls in for a sick day, or even slow days, EMTs must respond, all members of a crew are compassionate at/for the work they do, and yes, some more than others, for different reasons, but we can/should thank them every time there is an accident, slip and fall, car wrecks, distress calls for meds, and even med seekers who know who to call to get their fix for the night if they can't score on their own.

Calling an EMT to score meds is brave and stupid 'cause they normally have the police nearby or just a phone call away...so why risk it? Those are some of the calls they deal with on a regular basis, things we take for granted because we don't see what really happens before, during, and after the ambulance comes and goes. These stories and others are just some of the heroic acts I see as the husband, father, friend and sometimes helper to EMTs and drivers that live in this small town, many other people may have stories such as mine to tell but putting one's thoughts on paper takes more than the idea of doing it, it takes commitment on one's part to share his/her experiences with the world.

Most people never see the day-to-day course of life they must endure to save others, the stresses of many training hours, making sure crew and machine are in running order and everyone has the mental make-up to do their jobs without question and to the best of their abilities. This job doesn't discriminate, saving a life is just...it's not a game, no amount of money, power or privilege means nothing when you're dying or scared of dying without the help of others 1st on the scene to assess, medicate and transport to the nearest hospital. I was told that this is a thankless job and those that do it only seek the joy of seeing that person in a week or so, after his/her injury has gone away and they can express their appreciation in person.

The joy of someone being able to say "Thank you for saving my life" and mean it because without EMTs to the rescue one might be dead or in the hospital hooked up to a machine of some sort as a matter of living out one's life like a TV set. There's no amount of money that equals to the saving of a life, according to those who do this sort of thing for a living, EMTs live on the edge of sorts meaning, there is a rush about answering the call to save a life and the positive stories and experience that goes with it, something they can share at the end of the week or to a rookie looking to get into the business of saving lives.

We all know that every job isn't full of wine and roses but learning something that could save a life is priceless, because it may save an EMT's life if things were reversed to which are the worst patients on the planet, other than doctors, hahaha. I love my EMT, now knowing her mental and physical abilities to stay abreast of all her needs to stay an EMT for her entire career. She had many career options like the rest of us, Anna chose a career other than sports to which she is welcomed with open arms, she has a calming ability to take control of a situation, college isn't for everyone, yes, she has some college credits, but not enough to make her president of a university but enough to understand what she is reading or writing and way more than enough to save a life the first time around.

She is never questioned about her abilities, while others pick her brain all the time, about medicines to administer, whether a patient really needs to go to the hospital or just attention for an hour, things that require common sense too. Some things just come naturally to some, while others have trouble from beginning to end, this is a good problem to have, she will be sorely missed if she ever decided to retire and leave all she knows to someone else.

The complex world of EMTs and drivers are living and working in a scared-shitless world, they must act first then react second, eager doesn't mean smart, or having common sense which is at a premium with some of her junior crew members, so why would someone join an outfit to which lives are at stake every time out and not want to be able to handle every situation that comes along or when the alarm sounds?

Not Worth the Effort

Most recently Anna and her staff were invited to a Bar-B-Que and EMT of the year ceremony and everyone on the Northside of the county thought that Anna was a shoe-in for this award and those on the Southside of the county were jealous of her but as usual this was not to be. The south-siders were clueless of the time and effort Anna has/had put in, but at the Bar-B-Que things were different, the award went to a part-time EMT working full time for an Oil & Fuel Company here within the county, this guy was given the award because he works in the local area and is friends with those people on the awards committee, and not all those up for the award was evaluated to really pick the best person for the award and not someone's close friend.

Part of the Bar-B-Que was an extraction class (getting someone out of a smashed vehicle while still alive) and not kill them in the process, given by the local fire department and for all to participate in and use the tools, to know how to use them when a training session turns real out on the highway and when the conditions aren't the best. The awards committee had made up their minds as to who the winner of this award over five months would be ago but kept a lid on the winner's name until the Bar-B-Que and thus leaving all crew members North and South bound in the dark and guessing. They turned a two-ceremony into a nine-hour event if it were not for the ex-traction class, not all that were invited showed up even though it was not a mandatory event, the fireman gave the class and Anna was the patient to be removed after the fake accident scene and she is not the smallest person in the world to be removed from a vehicle by removing the door on the passenger side.

Anna and I discussed what would happen if she just decided to leave and work for another outfit, away from Carbon County, I can hear the locals complaining from here, but this only proves how two-faced these people are, and how they want your job but will never say it to your face and then act surprised when it happens, as we went to bed that night I asked Anna would she really think about getting another job doing the same thing except with different people who seem to like, respect, and look forward to working with her every day because of her reputation as a good to excellent EMT. I got no answer that night, but I did put the thought of "what if I…" on her mind, for at least one night.

I think she has been pushed to the edge of getting really pissed off at someone or something to force her hand, but knowing others are hoping you come and join them is a good feeling when and if she decides to leave, but Grace would be left to take control of a position she may not be ready for or want. They would have to ask her, while knowing that Anna has made up her mind to start over somewhere else. Anna's crew are set in their ways and are very comfortable knowing that Anna is around to clean up their messes and there are too many to count with their inability to process the good and the bad from every situation, to which Anna is called to either help or fix the most recent problem of that day or week. This has got to stop, because no one stays with one single job forever, and with this in mind, one must be ready for when that day comes whether from the top of the chain of command or someone near or at the bottom. There is no influx of new blood coming from another state or even a local high school kid looking for something new to do, or a transfer from another rig crew coming to Anna's aid, she is at the tip of her career point. At some point, they all get burned out, quit, or retire, but there must be new blood at some point to replace them or the rigs will stop rolling to the aid of others when the alarm sounds.

As I sit here and writer what needs to be said, the eyes of my wife fill with tears from another fall and lose of balance due to pain in her neck, to which her physical therapist Mycah says will go away over time but she doesn't believe him, 12 weeks of getting ground up like a burger does not seem like fun for anybody and the only good coming from this is that the government is paying for it. With her birthday, a few weeks away she got her presents early this year due to the fact that a few years past was on the light side of gift giving, a custom-made portrait and a brand-new/used truck should help me recover ever so nicely, it's kind of hard to treat your wife as she should be treated when we both are dealing with medical issues that could that one of us away from the other.

With all the things going on at work, she still can look forward to waiting for the alarm to sound so she can jump into action like she always has and do her job without thinking about the pain she has been in for the past two years or so with neck, arm, and shoulder injuries, which can be a pain in the ass for those in the medical field or an EMT who is always on call, even on her days off due to her crew not being the best of apples in the bush. She is plaining another trip out of county, at her own expense for a seminar weekend five hours away per trip but is too be present and accounted for when it starts that preceding Saturday morning after she arrives with Grace in tow for mental and physical support and to split the bills they both are forced to listen to others speak about things this town will never agree to or buy for future EMTs or drivers who still say that saving lives is a respectable career.

Most of the kids that live in this town can't wait to leave because there's nothing keeping them from leaving, most teenagers do have plans and almost none of them want to do what Anna and Grace do for a living even though they will be taught by the best EMTs this side of the county, teenagers must find themselves before they come back with an open mind and the ability to do. Most of them will never come back, and our daughter may be one of them but she also said she loves what her mom does and wants to do the same when she becomes old enough and hopes her mom will be doing the teaching when the time comes.

In the most recent of days Grace's life has changed for the better in my eyes because she was let go in her real job to which was a shock to the rest of us, because we thought she was a staple to the banking profession, the word on the street was her boss had someone waiting in the wings but only if there was a spot for the newbie. We gave Grace something to think about when we found out ourselves, like talking time off for the summer and then look for a new job when it starts to get cold and that's early October here, or ask for more hours with Anna as she will work all summer long except for a few days here and there, and we all know that Anna and Grace can work together, unlike some of her other crew members, who seem to not be able to do anything on their own without worry, concern, or regret when done with a task. As I had written before, Anna and Grace are true best of friends and need each other whether they know it or not, friends help each other when the time of need is greatest. Grace's current position is open to search for something new, to her regret, but sometimes a change is just what one may need if life is at a current standstill. I hope if things were reversed, the outcome would be the same, my close friend coming to my aid.

Still having trouble with Trudy, and hoping she would retire, and yet she still hangs around and takes other people's call time, and always assuming she's on duty and when not, and is now being tested as to her abilities to work as an EMT/driver is coming to the forefront. Anna has finally convinced her chain of command that Trudy is a liability and at some point, get someone killed due to her inability to act in the proper way in order to save a life over taking one.

Anna and I took Grace with us to her scheduled doctor's visit to confirm or deny if she has another dislocated right shoulder, either way Anna will be on a limited schedule for a while, for a few weeks to a month or two and yet surgery is not at all out of the question for the third time if I recall. They claim it's just a sprain to which will take some time to heal on its own if she just sits around the house and does nothing...not likely to happen. Things like this happen to those EMTs who lift 400-pound truck drivers from what is left of a smashed vehicle when they come through Wyoming at breakneck speeds to which is not the norm in California or other states to which the state speed limits are 75 mph or less. EMTs' silly season is mostly wintertime, when the speeds are reduced but thinking one can drive through a snowstorm with no weather warning goes up, those who can't drive in deep snow, high winds, black ice, wild animals that can cross your driven path at a moment's notice, or just a run-of-the-mill 50-car accident on the interstate is where

Anna and her crew get to work, along with the state troopers who are their first, they call for EMTs when accidents can and do turn fatal.

I can see us going back to the doctor's office in a few weeks because those steroid shots normally don't work and the pain is long lasting, which limits one's ability to work through that kind of pain, Anna and Grace do push each other to do will, study, and make themselves better so others may follow and while lightening the mood of their personal situations. On this Sunday morning it happened again, Anna was having a lazy day doing laundry and having breakfast when the alarm went off, she quickly found something appropriate to put on that represents her abilities and strength, and with a hand wave and a loud "I love you" she was out the door and with no timeframe for her return she could be gone all day. These are the type of days I wish to express to the world, those who answer the call in the despair of others, who does one muster up the courage to run into versus out of a life-altering situation, seeing adversary at the start of your day and holding serve on what comes before them by way of a life-and-death act.

A POSSIBLE CAREER CHANGE?

Just like when a cop has been on the beat too long and has mentally checked out some time ago and yet his body still goes through the motion day after day, he's looking for the ultimate excuse to confirm his real thoughts and fears well, Anna has the same problem of sorts. When we 1ˢᵗ moved out here to Wyoming we both had jobs in mind that would further our careers, but mine fell short, with 2 degrees and a military disability I could never be the cop/detective I so hoped of being.

Anna's mindset too is to serve the people of this town, one way or the other, the town mayor is about as effective as a pig working on a car, being available to the townspeople when they need him is nonexistent, his office hours are from 8 A.M. – 10 A.M. Monday through Friday and he can't be reached for comment the rest of the week, so to say he's useless is very common among those who need to see him on political matters and/or if he's running for another term in office. We even hope to get lied to over the phone and over the next 8 months till the next election we will have to put up with him.

Anna has been offered a chance to get him out of office, if she runs in his place, she already has the support of the older generation of people who see this town as a place to retire and to where things are very laid back and slow, and this is the start of something better. While driving to an appointment last week Anna asked me what did I think about her running for office when the time came. I explained to her that I was all in on the idea as her campaign manager and the fact that during the last election she only lost by a few votes and a lot of people were shocked that she didn't win the first time around and if the opportunity arose. Of one of her many (off-duty) jobs is board member to help promote this town for those who don't live here and yet want to stay. One should consider the location of which we live, one town 45 min. way to the east, another town 100 miles to the west of us via the interstate connecting all of us. Things are scarce here, so having a lot is not an option, Anna's connections outside this town can and will help others to see this place for what it can become, while bringing funds to buy and build here, instead of going elsewhere with people but less space to start anew and with less business competition pending on the products one has to sell, and with a population of less than 800 there are enough people here to tell one knows if his/her product(s) will sell here. As I had hoped, things have come to ahead for Trudy, she has had more chances to become the title she holds, an EMT. From where I sit she has caused more problems over the past two years than possible, she claims to be something she's not and if you question her the automatic answer was/is "I was not trained to do that" or "I don't know" and to the contrary on the latter, she went to as many classes, conferences, or meetings just like everyone else who are inclined to advance in their individual careers. Trudy doesn't need the money because her deceased husband worked for more than thirty years in the train industry, and she is also retired from teaching, so along with other monies coming in on a regular basis she should be retired and living in Florida somewhere, but she is meddling in the business of a younger crowd and out of league when it comes to saving the life of another. Trudy believes that she is not the problem with the crew, to which Anna is the station manager, and Grace is her number 1 in her absence, Trudy has on more than on occasion told others about victims' injuries and/or medical histories to people who don't need to know it.

Anna has finally come to the same conclusion as many others have seen or heard for themselves, that Trudy is unfit to work in the public eye and should be removed from such a workforce before she gets or causes someone's death, to which she will blame any and everyone within earshot. The chain of command has also come to this conclusion over the past few weeks, while out on the highways of this state and asked Trudy to simple tasks either for or to an accident victim, in which her response was something to the effect, "Anna didn't show me how to do that." That excuse has run out for

Trudy and in the back of her mind lying to get her way will cost her the job she claims she is good at, there are no plans to replace her according to Anna, to which is on another road trip to get businesses to come here and spend money or create a better atmosphere than what is here now.

TRUDY GETS THE MESSAGE

After many chances with Anna and others she can beg or cry her way to staying on as an EMT/Driver, Trudy has better late than never been reduced to "trainee," which means she's at the bottom of the food chain and has to do whatever is asked of her without question, in order to stay part of the team as a whole. Her demotion has come as no surprise to the rest of the crew and has been sorely needed from the inception, while Trudy got her EMT card through manipulation and good or bad timing depending on whom you ask. Anna still has issues with Trudy, even though she thinks she has done nothing wrong, and thinks she deserves to be in charge, to which no one will follow, respect her, or plans to work under her, if one could avoid it. Trudy still follows Anna and others when they are off-duty around town, trying to gather info she can use to benefit her position or cause in the EMT/Driver world. Anna, Grace and one other are planning a much-needed trip to Las Vegas in a month or so, to decompress from all the things they go through on an everyday basis. Anna is supposed to be saving money for this trip, I'm not sure if she is or I will have to help her out in that aspect, but I'm sure I will, the seminar they are going to is to help them attract businesses to come to Hanna, and try to relax, Anna has a knack for hitting the slot machines and winning money like she did several years ago when we were in the Bahamas while we were in the Navy coming back from a Med Cruise. We have never been to Las Vegas as a couple or as a family, nor have we ever been invited to go to such a place, and yes, we are close enough to go on our own but planning a trip such as this we will need extra money to spend, and hope we win more than gas money in a place where winning is at a premium.

Over the past few weeks the planning stages of our trip have changed along with Anna's work, Trudy has been suspended and is now reduced to a trainee with no power and limited skills to tell anyone what to do, nor can she be in charge. She still rides the coattails of Anna and hopes to be in her shoes one day, which will never happen because she lacks the people and ambulatory skills to help others without asking "how do I do that," it's just like a doctor saying "I don't know" to a patient.

Anna was again asked if she will run for mayor of this small town when the time comes, she was asked by the next town's newspaper editor because he knows how hard she has been working to make this town better by herself, other local board members have been asking for a few months now till the next election, she still has not decided as to her intentions but I hope she does run because as mayor she will have the ability to let other companies come here to see how a laid-back town can operate and function.

Anna's future is not locked down yet, whether she goes for a political position or moves up the chain of command into a better position than the one she's in right now. Trudy is still around and being a pain in the ass more than ever because she's reduced to trainee over station manager like Anna is, and may be plotting something so she can stay around for whatever is coming.

ONCE IN A LIFETIME

In a few days, an event will take place that will happen every one hundred years or so, and if you're alive to see it, it will be fantastic for most and a situational nightmare for a crew that is already on thin ice personnel wise, Anna and her crew along with all the others within the state must prepare for this event, which will cross the state in the middle of the night, so many out-of-towners will be coming through the state, city, county, and town to get a good parking spot to be witness to a "solar eclipse" for the first time in most of their lives. I have been on this earth for fifty-two years so far and I had never seen a solar eclipse, so one can imagine the excitement and surprise when it happens two days, it must seem like the "Beatles are coming" again. I can't see what the big deal is all about, it's a science thing that will last for all of twenty minutes, but the travelling into the state will generate as much money as if the Super Bowl was in town, people are planning their vacations around it, and parking will be first come first serve and almost anywhere one can get during the night. One can only guess what they will see with the naked eye in the middle of the night but if one is lucky enough to get those special glasses to see the eclipse without burning your retina if you stared at it too long, to which we all know is dangerous, I've never ever heard of anyone having to go to the hospital over this but if it's a thing, it's a thing. The other crews of three or more are at the ready for this event, but the stresses of this event are very high, because every EMT, Fireman, Driver, Asst. Driver, Policeman in the state will be up for the next 36-48 hours straight to be ready for every type of incident that could happen, major and minor, and the salary increase is a plus for most and necessary because they deserve it and more if it were possible to give them the extra money for an event like this. Usually only one or two crew units would be available for this type of thing but since it involves the whole country everyone who can be available will be, and most of them are just like the regular citizens who want to see the eclipse but not have all the trouble that may come. The police are in a different mindset, they expect trouble, and most of them look forward to locking up out-of-towners or charging them double the fines and/or court dates if the local jails get full. On the medical side of things, it's more of hurry up and wait, something will happen, it's just a matter of what level and how much, I would think they would want to be busy over this versus just waiting in a stationary position while the eclipse is happening or waiting for the out-of-towners to leave. The eclipse went off with all the splendor of a science miracle for all of us that has never seen an eclipse before, to which most of us has not. The EMTs, drivers, firemen, and policemen waiting for something bad to happen had to wait longer than usual besides one or two minor events, the eclipse was a success, most people from across the state enjoyed what they were a witness to. It was an event for a generation of people to see and talk about at the dinner table, express one's awe of something we will never see again in one's lifetime, the sun and the moon are wondrous creatures too and if they want to get close enough to see each other face to face then all we can do is watch from miles away. I was in amazement for what we saw, it was bright and moving with the grace of a young dancer while being hot enough to kill all that crosses her path without some sort of protection.

People have left as quickly as they have arrived to see nature's spectacle, all the hustle and bustle of the big city in one day's worth of excitement and in a flash, it's gone and so are all the onlookers and people trying to capture the event on film or in picture form. The EMTs were uber ready for some sort of mass casualty event that would send them into a medical frenzy that would last for days on end. In a twist of fate, the event went off without a problem, I would imagine it's better to be prepared and nothing happens vs. not being prepared and have the world come crashing down all around them and people end up hurt, dying or even dead. In better news the girls were off to Las Vegas for another EMT conference for a week, but the timing was/is a little more dangerous now in the aftermath of what happened two weeks before, an armed gunman from the hotel across the street to where the girls are staying, from his hotel room he had the advantage of height, fire power, and being unknown. From what the reports after the event had happened they said he planned the event the week before by placing his weapons in his room one gun at a time till his assortment of firepower was in place and no one was the wiser due to his comings and goings, we heard he had a girlfriend to whom he sent back to the Philippines with $500, she had her known problems too, being married to two other men while using 3 different social security numbers and not telling her current boyfriend what was going on in her life.

But our shooter is the focus right now, his background is unknown to most but the ones that do know him say he's every emotional, unpredictable, rich and follows in his father's footsteps, to which he was an escape artist from several departments of corrections from back in the 60s and 70s. Our shooter was mad as hell at someone or something but he took his anger out on a crowd full of people whom he had no personal contact, the unsuspecting people below him were at an open-air concert and had no idea of what their lives will now become in just a few minutes' time, when the shooting started most of the concert goers were thinking that the firing was part of the show, but it was not and once the crowd goers noticed that the shots were coming from above them and it was for a few nonstop minutes and from two different directions, it meant he was moving from room to room and shooting at all the people he could. This put people into a panic as they started running to safety and wondering why would someone shot at them for no real reason, in his hotel hallway a security guard heard what was going on and did his best to get the shooter's attention by banging on his door to get him to stop, it worked to a point, the shooter came to the door with anger in his heart and shot the security guard at point-blank range but before he went up to the shooter's room he called the police to inform them of what is happening at this hotel and the floor the shots were coming from, once reinforcements showed up to the room and as they entered, the shooter shot himself in the head to the horror of all the policemen who were there to stop and arrest this gunman with a hidden agenda.

Anna and Grace still wanted to go and had no choice but to go to Las Vegas in the weeks after this horrible event, the shooter did this on purpose and wanted to kill as many people as possible and as quickly as possible, for the reason(s) we will never know because he took the coward's way out of this situation and took the innocent with him. Those people who died never thought that on that day would be their last, they never thought to say good-bye to their loved ones for the last time, held them close, kissed their spouse(s), boy or girlfriends, confirmed they had a will or was even feeling sick enough to go out for a night on the town. They had no idea that things would change forever and those people that did survive would be scared in an altogether separate way and ask did they survive while others were killed in a hail of gunfire from a man with no personal connection to them at all.

LET'S GET PERSONAL

After having this job for 3-plus years and everything going as well as can be…it's gone. It was taken from her like a dirty blanket a child need not have anymore, Anna is more qualified than any of the fellow EMTs and yet one quick conversation with the station manager and Anna's out on her ear relegated to just an EMT in a town close to ours but far away enough to make a day of it workwise.

Others are upset they couldn't go on the Vegas trip, Anna and Grace had planned almost a year in advance, and the main culprit was Trudy, her whole mindset was or is to look for sympathy in every way possible, even telling her bosses and friends that she has cancer (breast) and gets upset when people ask her about it or the fact that she shows no signs of a disease that no one wants…ever.

The new EMT Maggie with less than 6 months of experience on the job and fresh out of training classes will now oversee seasoned EMTs who have seen more than Maggie will in a year's time. Maggie is a local neighbor, the opportunity for one of fifteen people in the five areas to work as the Hanna-Station manager and the bonus of $100 per month. We can assume that the powers to be didn't have the courage to say at the last meeting that they wanted to go in a different direction leadership wise and tell Anna and her staff why.

Management sees less money over experience the better of the two, a fresh set of eyes from a person who doesn't see what experience does, the council of 5 to 7 people who on a regular basis never sees what EMTs do or have never had to extricate a person from a crash scene thought a newbie was/is good enough to save a life without being scared shitless or manage a staff and vehicles. The normal timeframe for a newbie to become experienced enough to ride along with experienced EMTs and/or a driver assistant is six weeks the normal time for probation, a double standard runs deep.

A kind of newbie Anna and Grace can trust is a guy named Kyle, he works well with everyone but Maggie because she's new and don't understand the non-verbal clues when to do versus when to ask, Kyle is part time because of his other interests bear loving photographer. All the rules should apply to everyone not just the ones who benefit the most, junior people should know what to do and not be told all the time, it makes the junior person and the trainer look bad if simple actions are questioned, or that junior person can't be trusted to act the way an EMT, assistant, or driver should in the time of need for a victim.

It's Over...Now What?

After a few weeks of back-and-forth about the situation that most people do to unwind after a long day's work of saving lives...having a drink to calm nerves, rehash the day's events, try to remember or forget the harsh reality of things happening on this city's streets and highways. Many people are pissed off at the entire scope of things that happened to some of the best EMTs in the state, Anna is well respected but fragile right now because she thinks that there is nothing else she can do for work other than save perfect strangers on a regular basis. The three of them were fired, over one incident that happens at the end of a shift worldwide when it comes to relaxing in a stressful job to where lives are in the balance, many of Anna's well-wishers are shocked and are willing to offer her the opportunity to work with or for them in another capacity.

Just like most of the world today, when things go wrong and it's not your fault you sue the bastards, so basically half of the EMTs are willing to go to court over getting fired due to the powers that be power tripping and are scare to do the right thing over having the balls to make his own decision with the evidence, or lack thereof, using judgment and reason. Her voice is cracked, eyes are watering up over the thought of not being an EMT anymore, tough on the outside and tender hearted to a fault, the board that made this horrible decision will soon feel the power of emptiness when the next big accident hits the highways of this fair state and there is no one to call and responded, no calming voice to say "Everything will be okay" or a victim saying "I know you, I'm glad you're here to help." Experience at anything is a wonderful thing, no words need to be said in order for things to happen in a positive manner, or when a person is out of control and needs to be calmed down with the proper medication. EMTs know how to do these things and more with just eye contact to keep control of the situation and everyone gets what they need at the of the shift.

The local lawyers will have a good time prosecuting a Politician, who is a bully and uses his size to intimidate others into doing what he thinks is right without thinking or using proper judgment from his fellow Board members, in Anna's case along with others, the vote was supposed to be unanimous in order to fire a group of people to which several were not even on duty on the night in question, while Anna took herself off duty because she had one drink, told the supervisor of such, and was ordered to go home in the event of a call, to which nothing happened that night, which in my eyes made everything ok and safe for others.

Now seven people in all will leave the EMT/Fire Department due to one man's inability to listen, judge fairly, not be power hungry, or intimidation by position. This Board member now has a law suit coming and doesn't even know it, others around him knew this was a onetime mistake, and that over seven years as an EMT Anna and her crew were exceptional at what they walk out the door, leaving the department helpless and hopeless. With what is left now, the department will not last

A Second Chance at Something Good

It's been a while since all the unnecessary noise was heard in this town over something as less exciting as a prostate exam, the powers that be had to make a statement as to what they were and weren't going to do by way of EMTs, drivers, and other staff members, so Anna and others felt it for the past few months. Some of them were let go while some got their jobs back but under very different circumstances like having to start their careers all over again, nobody would in their right mind do this, but work is work.

Anna was one of the lucky ones to get the benefit of this, owe so gracious new but old positions back with the EMT staff, but she has the option of moving on from them as a whole, but to me she still can't make up her mind without leaving her best friend Grace behind, to which things aren't go appealing by way of job offers or being able to go back to her old job without getting dirty looks and stares from the new management because they heard about the old situation without knowing all the details or having an objective option about what had gone on.

Anna did her footwork to find another job either at the local hospital or the wind farms, yes, both different from being an EMT, but a new career move may be what she needs...a fresh start doing something else but with the same energy as before. She may over time be in a position of power on her own to rehire Grace and others if they want to try something else as well.

The money and hours are something to behold when you're looking for almost anything, and as they say "beggars can't be choosers," so I hope she makes up her mind soon, the less stress we both have the better considering my situation too, but that's for another day. She held that bit of information from me until today, for reasons I'm not too sure about but it surely puts a hold on our vacation, but I'd rather have her working too versus sitting around giving me an ear full for no reason sometimes and thus a fight breaks out, not good for either of us or the family as a whole.

This would be a second chance at something good for all the right reasons if she follows through with the new opportunities that has come her way, many others aren't so fortunate. The stresses of not knowing if one has a job or not can be daunting, Anna is still waiting for one of her closest friends to inform her of the news, personal things have been put on hold for now, but things can change in a flash.

Going Back...Not an Option

It has come to Anna's attention that going back to work for the town's Ambulance service is not going to happen, whether her hook-ups speak on her behalf or not, at this point she is on her own (work wise), they both were two of the four people left in the cold over an incident only two of them were on duty to get a reprimand over.

Both Anna and Grace were recently waiting on a grace period by the new board members to decide whether to bring them all back but instead they went in a different direction...which means they're out. Luckily Anna wasn't fully entwined in that hope of going back so her instincts were correct to look elsewhere for work. Classes for EMT work isn't cheap or local and understanding this concept also helps in getting signed off on the paperwork or card is a must, this proves what you know and for how long one has been working in the EMT/Ambulance world.

I hear that moving from one state to another while working in the EMT field may or may not meaning starting over...EMT basic but one can't lose knowledge even if moving but money and benefits. I wonder what others think of this as a non-option. I wonder what others would do if the situation was reversed, moving on from your dream job with no real outlook into the future makes one possibly rethink their job. I would imagine that there would be some sort of verbal fight or even furniture moving if they had to move on with nothing to fall back on.

We all know that time waits for no one, and moving into a new career doesn't work well for many people, it's just like a career service member having to get out of the service they love and have spent most of their lives doing or striving to become good to better than others at doing and with things beyond your control it's over.

Booze Never Lies

After a traumatic event how does one decompress? Cops, firemen and EMTs/Paramedics see all kinds of things no one should ever seeing again, but the mental image is still around months even years later after the event has passed. I was told from Anna that the worst thing she has seen was an accident that involved someone she knew, which made helping her even more important and stressful. By the time Anna and her crew arrived on scene…it was too late, her friend was gone.

Later that week all the EMT crews within the state were in a somber mood for the loss of their friend and neighbor, so how does someone deal with a loss that close to home? Some drink and tell a little truth as they become buzzed, some keep it all to themselves, some do it in combinations (drink, talk, cry), Anna told me that every time she sees an 18-wheeler she has a flashback to the event in question. Most of the people that fit into this realm as a special breed of person to run into the action vs. running away from it, military included, as we were both former military personnel.

We can let our emotions get the best of us in the worst of times, by yelling and throwing things, or asking ourselves "why?" but in the back of our minds we really know why but things get out of hands quick. Some of us can't process traumatic actions, it just seems to never go away, or pops in our minds at the least inopportune time and makes us rekindle bad events all over again. I know when I was in the Navy during (OIF) Operation Iraq Freedom things were tense and we all were scared but most of us didn't show it until we were alone with our thoughts. EMTs and others can't show signs of weakness in the eyes of the victims they are inline to help or freezing up at the sight of blood or worse.

As part of their training they work shifts at the local hospital in order to get used to the things they are about to see and do in the field of EMT work. The woman whose job she took from Anna is coming back to haunt her, she like the power of being in charge but not all the details like, paperwork after a scene, others during a not so good of a job helping the victim, or being available on down time to cover the town she lives in. She doesn't know that the word spreads faster than a teenage rumor at high school, her chain of command doesn't hear all the gory details of how things went wrong but the locals do and even though she's new, they want her out and Anne wants back in, so the senior citizens will feel comfortable knowing that if something were to happen to them they would have a better-than-average chance of survival.

The old gang is gone, Anne has options that she can't pass up, Grace is just waiting for the phone to ring, their driver is out altogether due to health reasons, demotion, lack of hours as a whole and being at the bottom of the food chain, and the last member of Anna's crew is too out altogether but for a totally different reason, she has become an attention hound and has laid claim to having cancer and other personal issues just to be in the middle of a conversation or two.

Social media is not a kind place to lay false claim to something as harsh as cancer, there are others whose day starts and ends in pain of the worst sorts, plus the many pills and feeling like today is it, no one should claim to be ill when they are not, and thus having to lie when the symptoms don't show. Anna's ex-friend is doing just that due to a fallout over their friendship on the ambulance service and who's the lead EMT.

One cannot help who likes them the best or least in the world Ambulatory work, you hope they all do as you try to save a life in a stressful situation like a car crash, the victim doesn't care who comes as long as they do. As I was thinking about the victims, it happened the alarm sounded as she was off and running but not as an EMT but a fireman, on this day while on scene of an accident a trucker saw that his time was more valuable than all others, so he saw fit to drive through an accident scene at more than 60 mph. The scene was rental car versus 18-wheeler...guess who won if you call surviving a head-on collision winning, the car torn to shreds but the victim lived to pay for her now destroyed rental car.

This is just the average day of one of the most dangerous jobs in the world, and not many people know that it's life and death for all involved not just the victims.

What is a boring day at your job? Think for a minute what a boring day to an EMT means, "No one died today on my watch," a trip to the hospital maybe but not the feeling of helplessness when you do all you can, and they still die.

PAYING FOR THAT RIDE

The price of an ambulance ride can be high, on average it's between $20 to $75k, and that's in a town as small as ours and that's because if you need a helicopter ride to the hospital from the accident scene it really is life and death, or you can refuse sign a statement and take your chances on your own…you decide. Did you know that the ambulance or EMTs can't refuse anybody, you call them they come every time without question, policemen have options when it comes to arresting people and depending on the situation too, EMTs don't.

EMTs have frequent callers who are looking for a daily fix, a ride to the hospital for the night, attention from others, or really looking to get clean but don't know how to start, or all the above in a single day or week. Certified EMTs and (A/Is) advanced and intermediates are the only ones allowed to give medications to a victim while in route to a hospital pending on the victim's pain level and/or to sedate the victim for the helicopter ride itself.

I was told that it may take a while to pay off that bill, but I would imagine that it's money well spent.

About the Author

Joseph E. Fowler Jr. is new to the literary scene with a new and exciting prospective look at the world of an EMT/Firefighter that his wife has lived for the past few years. His insight into this world can run all over the emotional scale. This is the author's first work. We hope he continues to entertain you.